MASTER
BUILDER

HACKS FOR
MINECRAFTERS

MASTER BUILDER

HACKS FOR MINECRAFTERS

THE UNOFFICIAL GUIDE TO TIPS AND TRICKS THAT OTHER GUIDES WON'T TEACH YOU

MEGAN MILLER

Sky Pony Press
New York

Copyright © 2014 by Hollan Publishing, Inc.

Minecraft® is a registered trademark of Notch Development AB

The Minecraft game is copyright © Mojang AB

Sky Pony Press books may be purchased in bulk at special discounts for sales promotion, corporate gifts, fund-raising, or educational purposes. Special editions can also be created to specifications. For details, contact the Special Sales Department, Sky Pony Press, 307 West 36th Street, 11th Floor, New York, NY 10018 or info@skyhorsepublishing.com.

Sky Pony® is a registered trademark of Skyhorse Publishing, Inc.®, a Delaware corporation.

Minecraft® is a registered trademark of Notch Development AB.
The Minecraft game is copyright © Mojang AB.

Visit our website at www.skyponypress.com.

10 9 8 7 6 5 4 3 2 1

Printed in China

Library of Congress Cataloging-in-Publication Data is available on file.

Cover photo credit Megan Miller
Book design by Sara Kitchen

Print ISBN: 978-1-5107-3803-4
Ebook ISBN: 978-1-5107-4390-8

TABLE OF CONTENTS

INTRODUCTION

Half of playing Minecraft is building—building shelters, bases, traps, and farms. Some people like building so much with Minecraft's blocks that that's pretty much all they do. Minecraft fans have built amazing things, joining up in teams to build intricate and massive structures like the space shuttle, fully detailed cities with hundreds of buildings, bridges, and parks, as well as epic scenes and buildings from *Lord of the Rings*, *Harry Potter*, and more. To see some of these, search online for "amazing Minecraft buildings."

For most people, though, building means a simple cube of cobblestone, with a couple panes of glass. Of course, if you're busy killing zombies and raising cows, building a snazzy home may be on the bottom of your list. You may find it more important to have a protective wall that a creeper can't explode.

However, if you have an architectural streak and you want to get started on building awesome homes and buildings in your Minecraft world, this book will show you the tricks the Minecraft experts use, including:

- How to build arches and spheres that look curved

- How to use depth and detail to make your buildings look realistic

- How to use steps, levers, trapdoors, and more for your furniture and amenities

To help you get started on some no-fail, amazing builds, this book will show you how to plan a basic house and customize it 6 different ways.

You'll also find step-by-step guides for building:

- An airship

- A fortified castle

- A glass dome

- A pagoda

- An underwater house

Building in Minecraft can be much more than making a shelter to keep you safe at night. If you like, you can spend time in Creative mode and take the time to build amazing things. In addition to homes, you can build almost anything you can find in the real world.

Blocks to Build With

You can basically build with any blocks, of course.

Traditional building materials. Traditional building materials are stone (including diorite, andesite, and granite), stone bricks,

bricks, cobblestone, logs of the six different tree types and their wood planks, and sandstone. There are several variations on some of these blocks, such as mossy stone bricks, polished granite, and chiseled sandstone.

Traditional building materials that you can craft and find in Survival mode easily include stone, cobblestone, sandstone, bricks, logs, planks, and their variations.

Other blocks to use. Other building blocks that are a bit harder to get, but make great building materials, are terracotta, glazed terracotta, concrete, glass, and dyed wool. Be careful with concrete powder though, as it has gravity, like sand, and will turn into regular concrete if it comes into contact with water blocks.

There are blocks from the Nether (quartz, nether brick, nether wart blocks, and red nether brick) and blocks from the End (purpur blocks and endstone), and the blocks you find in ocean monuments—prismarine, dark prismarine, prismarine bricks, and sea lanterns. But you don't have to stick with traditional materials—you can use giant red mushroom blocks, dry sponges, anything you want at all. You probably want to avoid building with gravel, concrete powder, and sand, as these can collapse. You should also avoid placing any flammable blocks within 4 blocks of a fire source, like lava. Flammable blocks can spread fire to other blocks and include wood, wooden items like fences, grass, vines, leaves, wool, carpet, hay, coal blocks, and bookshelves.

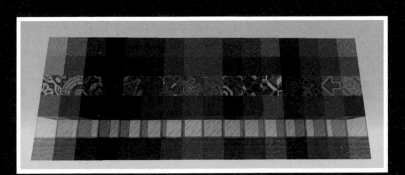

You can use the 16 color dyes to craft colorful wool, glass, terracotta and concrete for your buildings.

Experiment with all of Minecraft's building blocks. You can re-purpose many for other uses. Two trapdoors can be the side arms for a chair; a carpet can cover a table, floor, or chest to add color, End rods can be used as stairs; and a redstone lever can be a sink faucet.

Basic Building Steps

The basic steps to follow when you build something are:

- Decide what you want to build. If you can, use photos or pictures as references or for inspiration.

- Decide how big it's going to be and how much space you need. Draw a simple blueprint or layout on paper.

- Find a location in your world for your build.

- Clear a flat area to start building.

- Create foundations for a building or markers that show where you are placing the front, back, and sides of your building.

- Build! Build the outer general structure first. (For homes and buildings, this would be the walls, floors, and roof.)

- Detail and decorate. Go over your structure, correcting mistakes, making improvements, and adding the details like carpets, banners, and textured slabs that will bring your creation to life.

Building to Scale

If you are recreating something from real life in Minecraft blocks, at "real-life" size within Minecraft, each Minecraft block is defined as 1 meter cubed, or 3.3 feet in each direction. So if you want to build your own house in Minecraft, you can measure the walls in feet or meters and know about how many Minecraft blocks it will take. You can't use half blocks in Minecraft, of course, only whole ones, so you will need to round up or down for the Minecraft measurement. For example, if my house is 45 feet wide by 30 feet deep, I'd divide by 3 to get the number of Minecraft blocks: 15 wide by 10 deep.

In Minecraft, 1 block is equivalent to 1 meter (or 3.3 feet) cubed in the real world. That means Steve is about 6 feet tall!

Building Giant Sizes

If you want to build a supersized version of something, find the real-world measurements and multiply them to get the final measurements. So if I wanted to build a giant skateboard, I would measure a real one in inches first—height, width, size of the wheels. This will give you the right proportions. Then you can build the skateboard in blocks instead of inches, or multiply all the measurements to make the design as large as you like.

Counting by Blocks

Many times in building something, you have to count the blocks you are using. You may need to make sure two walls are the same length or place two buildings the exact same size or distance from a third building. It's very easy to lose track of where you are when you're counting, or miss a block, or even get interrupted and forget. One way to keep track is to use some kind of marker every fifth block. That way, if you lose track, you can recount by fives to where you are.

Here are three ways to use counting markers: in a wall, place a different block every fifth block—you can go back to replace it later; punch a hole in the ground; or place a single block every five.

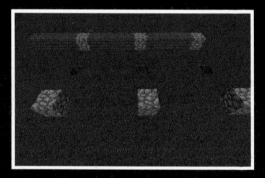

Building in Creative Mode

Building in Minecraft is much easier in Creative mode. In Creative mode, you have a never-ending supply of Minecraft blocks, so you don't need to plan on having the right materials. You can break blocks instantly with your hand. You can also fly around your building to place blocks, so you're in no danger of falling and damaging or killing yourself. And of course, mobs won't hurt you. With cheats on, you can change the time of day instantly so you can always work in daylight. You can also use the pick block key (usually the mouse's middle key) to select any block in your environment and put it in your hand, ready to place.

There are lots of advantages to building in Creative mode, like not being at risk of a long fall to the ground!

Building in Survival Mode

Although building in Creative mode is easier, building in Survival mode can be more satisfying. You have to do the work to locate, gather, and craft materials and plan efficiently so you don't waste these hard-won resources. You also feel pride when you have met the challenge of a time-consuming build accomplished in a hostile world.

So if you are up for the challenge of building in Survival mode, here are some tips:

- Build scaffolding from dirt blocks as you get higher. You can build dirt walkways and stairs outward from dirt beams to get to new places.

- Keep a stack of sand and a shovel so you can drop a pillar and shovel your way back down to the ground.

- If you are working really high above the ground, have a bucket of water (or a slime block) handy. For a long drop, you might just have enough time place water or slime on the ground before you hit it.

- Enchant your boots with feather falling to protect you from fall damage.

- Use the sneak key (Shift) with W and S so you can place blocks directly in front of you and underfoot.

In Survival mode, you can create a scaffold of dirt steps and beams to help you get to new heights.

In Survival, use the sneak key (Shift key) to creep over the edges of blocks. This allows you to place blocks in front of you at your feet and not fall to the ground. Hold the sneak key until you make it back to a solid block underfoot.

CHAPTER 2

MAKING CURVES AND ANGLES WITH SQUARE BLOCKS

Round castle towers, glass survival domes, airship balloons, and arched bridges all are built with curves and angles. However, Minecraft blocks are famously lacking these curves—it's a square, ninety-degree world. To overcome this building obstacle, Minecraft players have learned to approximate curves and angles so well that, at a distance, you can build a Minecraft Golden Gate Bridge that looks like the real thing!

Here are some techniques and ideas that will get you building arches, angles, and circles like a pro.

Diagonals and Angles

A diagonal line isn't straight up and down, but it's not a curve either. It's a straight line that moves at an angle. The angle of a diagonal line may be steep or shallow, but it remains the same angle along the whole line. It rises a specific number of blocks for each block it travels horizontally.

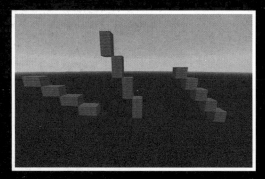

From left to right: a slightly angled or shallow line, a steep diagonal, and a 45 degree angle.

To make a steep line, for each block that you place sideways, go up 2, 3, 4 or more blocks. It's the opposite for a shallow angle. For each block you rise, go 2, 3, 4 or more blocks along. Keep the ratio (1:3 or 3:1) the same the whole way along the line.

Placing Blocks Diagonally

Many times when you are building, especially when building curves, you need to place blocks diagonally to each other without having them actually touching sides.

For a diagonal block that is touching along one edge: Place the first block, one or two temporary blocks above it or to one side, and the final diagonal block where you want it. Then destroy the blocks in between. If you're working in Survival mode, you may want to use a "cheap" block like dirt as a temporary block.

Use 1 temporary block to add a *diagonal* block along one edge, and then destroy the temporary block.

For a diagonal block that is touching just one corner: Do as above, but build out one more block from the top temporary block.

Use two temporary blocks to add a diagonal block that touches just one corner of another block, then destroy the two temporary blocks.

Curves

Whereas a diagonal or angled line keeps the same ratio of vertical to horizontal blocks as it goes, a curve changes the ratio. A curve can change slowly (a slight curve) or quickly (a steep curve).

To make a curve, you decrease the number of blocks that you place vertically (or horizontally) as you progress with almost every new step. (You can have a few steps that are angular, rather than curved, and still keep the overall curved look in Minecraft.)

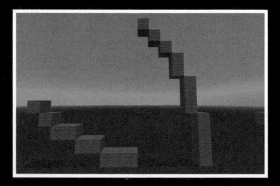

The first curve is made from 1 step of 3 blocks at the bottom, 2 steps of 2 blocks, and 2 steps of 1 block. The second curve is made from 1 step of 4 blocks, 1 step of 3, 1 step of 2, and 3 steps of 1.

Circles

The easiest way to make a circle in Minecraft is to follow a pattern for a circle and exactly copy the number of blocks. You can find many patterns for circles, ellipses, and spheres online by searching for "Minecraft circle, sphere, ellipse patterns." But there are some simple techniques you can use to make your own circles by hand that look just as good.

First you decide how big a circle you want, in terms of its diameter. The diameter is the length of a straight line from one side of the circle to the other that passes through the circle's center point. Half of the diameter is the radius. It's the line from the circle center to the edge. It is easiest to create a circle with one center block, which means that the diameter will always be an odd number.

Next, create a cross whose two lines are the length of the diameter.

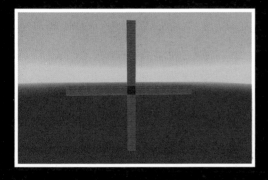

This cross is for a circle with a diameter of 15 blocks across.

At each end of the four spokes that come from the center, create four flat lines of the same length. The length of this line should be 5 blocks long for (odd) diameters of 9 to 17, 7 blocks long for diameters between 19 and 41, and 9 blocks long for diameters 43 to 49.

With a diameter of 15 blocks, spokes 5 blocks long are good. With the pink diameter block in the middle, you just add 2 blocks to either side for the total length of 5.

Once you've set the spokes, you'll need to make a curve in one corner of the circle. The curve needs to be symmetrical, so you can start by placing a line that is shorter than the spoke ends, starting from the spoke's end. Continue to shorten the additional lines until they meet at the center. You may need to experiment to make sure the quarter circle curve is symmetrical and looks good.

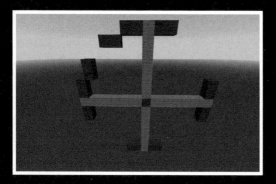

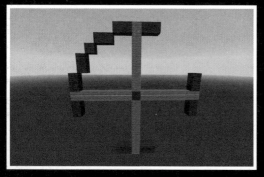

Start the curve by placing lines that are shorter than the length of the spoke ends. At the top, the line should be horizontal, and at the side, it should be vertical. For bigger circles, continue this way, decreasing the length of the lines till they meet in the middle. In this case, there is just one space left for a single block.

Once you've finished the quarter circle curve, copy it exactly to the other three parts of the circle.

Copy the curve pattern to the other three "corners" of the circle. If you don't want the center or the diameter in the finished circle, break those blocks.

You can use this basic technique to make circles of any size. Circles and arches can be replicated in Minecraft at small sizes, but they tend to look better and smoother the larger they are. A circle with a diameter of under 7 blocks tends to look more like a square.

Here are patterns for four circles with diameters of 13, 11, 9, and 7 blocks.

Arches

You'll want to use arches for making amazing bridges, majestic entryways, and building details. You can make an arch with a half circle on top of two straight sides, but you can also make arches that are wide, shallow, or pointy. The one thing to keep in mind as you build an arch is to maintain the curve; each new line of blocks in the curve should be shorter or the same length as the previous. When the curve changes to point the other direction, each new line of blocks should be the same length or longer than the previous.

Notice that an arch is symmetrical and that the curve for each side of an arch goes from decreasing vertical lines to increasing horizontal lines (3, 3, 3, 2, 1, 1, 2, 3). You can make arches that are wider than this, narrower, higher, or steeper.

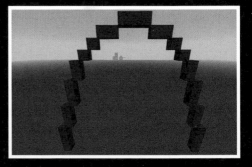

Spheres

Like circles, you can find patterns online that you can use to make spheres. You can make them yourself, although they are a bit harder than circles. In Minecraft, one way to make a sphere (or an ellipsoid) is by creating a series of circles placed one on top of the other. In the middle is the circle with the largest diameter, and as you move out from the middle, the circle diameter decreases, although the center has several circles of the same size. The tricky bit is that you don't decrease the size of the circle by a single block with each step. You need repeat circle sizes so that you create a curve as you decrease the circle size.

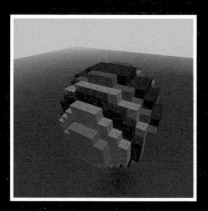

A sphere is essentially layers of smaller and smaller circles. When you make a sphere, you have to make sure that the slope created as the layered circles decrease in size (above, from the red circles to the smallest pink circle) is also a circle. This means that some circle layers will be repeated. In this sphere, the middle three red circle layers are identical.

To help you build a sphere, you can create an inner frame similar to the frame you created for a circle. This cross has a third bar showing the depth of the sphere. Then, around these three bars, you create identical circles. You can use these circles as a guide to the outside edges of the sphere as you fill in each layer of the sphere. It is easier to start with the horizontal middle and build up or down.

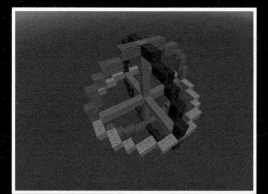

A frame for building a sphere. The central pink 3D cross shows the diameter of the sphere. Around this, you build three identical circles to show the curve of the outside of the sphere.

The sphere shape can be used for floating habitats, space ships, giant balls, and balloons. Often you will want to use just half a sphere shape to create domes for large towers, churches, mosques, and glass survival habitats.

Ellipses and Ellipsoids

Ellipses are flattened circles, and you can make them either by joining two arches together or using a central cross with one crosspiece shorter than the other. As with arches, you need to make sure each half is identical to the other. Ellipses can be used to help you make ellipsoids, which are elongated spheres. Ellipsoids can be used to make air ship balloons, sports stadiums, and more.

Use the same skills you use for making arches and circles to make ellipses.

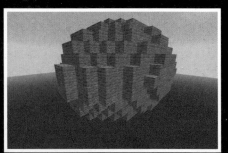

An ellipsoid is like an elongated sphere, and you can make it in the same way as a sphere. You can stack ever-decreasing circles on each othe or create a frame of ellipses and a 3 cross.

CHAPTER 3

DESIGNING AND PLANNING YOUR HOME

For building a simple, good-looking home in Survival mode that is beyond a basic cabin, but not a massive base or mansion, you can follow these steps.

1. Find your location.
Pick a relatively flat area for your home. You may want to be at the top of a hill for a view of your surroundings or by water, depending on how you like to play. Other things to keep in mind in selecting a location are:

(a) Clearing enough space for a defensive wall around your home.

(b) Clearing enough trees so that spiders and mobs can't jump over the wall or onto your roof.

(c) Deciding how much area you need around you for farming.

This location looks good for a simple house, with plenty of flat land good for farming and lots of animals.

2. Decide what rooms you need and how big they should be.
At the minimum, you will need to place a bed, your chests, your crafting table, and your furnaces. You'll want room for your enchantment table, bookcases, and anvil. If you're into potions, you'll need room for the brewing station, a Nether wart farm, and some internal source of water. The one area that will probably expand the most is the area for your chests, as you collect and mine more and more stuff.

So the minimum rooms and sizes you will want are:

- **Bedroom:** a room at least 3×3

- **Crafting room:** to fit a crafting table, two 3-high stacks of double chests, and two stacks of two furnaces, make a 5×6 room at least, with 4-block high walls

- **Enchantment:** to fit fifteen bookshelves, the enchantment table, and an anvil, make a 5x5 room

- **Potion room:** to fit a 4×4 infinite water pool, a small Nether wart farm, several stacked chests, and the brewing stand, make a 6×7 room

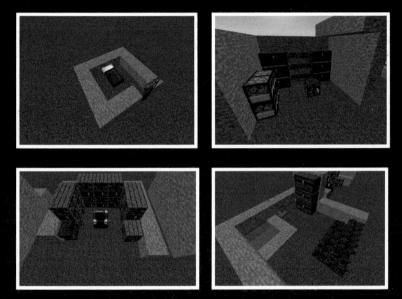

You'll want your home to be big enough for your activities: spaces for sleeping, crafting, enchanting, and if you're ready, brewing.

If you want to merge rooms so that you use one large room for crafting and enchantment, add the minimum space you need for all your gear for both activities. If you want to make everything a little more spacious, add 1–3 blocks in each direction.

You may also want to add rooms just for decoration and hominess, such as an entry hall, a bathroom, a kitchen, and a living room.

Make a list of all the rooms you want and about how big they should be. You can use paper and pencil to make a rough lay-out, with the number of blocks you think each room and its walls will take up.

3. Clear your location to make it ready for building.
Add or destroy ground blocks to make an even surface. Clear trees and make sure you have enough space for your house and other needs. In general, for a smaller house, you will probably need an area that is at least 30x30 blocks.

Building on a Slope

Although building on flat land is easiest, you can also build on slope. Just start by choosing what level at which you want to build your bottom floor and construct a foundation out from there to include the rooms you need. Cut into the slope if nec-essary, and build walls down from the foundation to the slope.

If you want to build on a slope, build out what will be the bottom floor of your house for a foundation. You can fill in underneath the slope as you like—with a rocky base, wood frames, or more hillside.

4. Decide if you want your home to have a particular style.
Popular styles include traditional, cabin or country, modern, and medieval. Use the following types of base wall block for these styles. (If you don't want to stick to a particular style, select one of the main wall-building blocks to start with.)

- **Traditional:** red brick

- **Cabin/Country:** wood planks (any type)

- **Modern:** stone, snow, or plain quartz block

- **Medieval:** for plaster walls, use sandstone or snow; for a stone base, use cobblestone

5. Blueprint your home.
Make a blueprint for your home. If you like, you can do this first on paper, outside the game, to make it easier to fix and make changes. When you are ready to blueprint in Minecraft, place lines of stone blocks in the grass to show the walls of the house and between rooms. Also mark out with a different colored block where windows will go. Leave spaces for where doors or entrances will be.

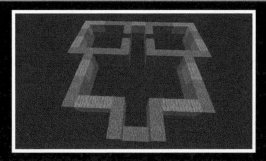

Here's a blueprint for a survival house using 2-block-high stone walls to show where the rooms are and blue wool to show where the windows will go. The entrance sticks out at the front, and there is a large room for crafting and chests. At the back will be a bedroom and a room for enchanting.

In general, the following layouts are typical for small homes in the following styles:

- **Traditional:** symmetrical or L-shaped

- **Cabin/Country:** square, rectangular, or L-shaped

- **Modern:** overlapping squares and rectangles (more than four corners!)

- **Medieval**: rectangular or L-shaped

Other things to take into account include:

- **Second floors and basements.** If you want to add additional floors or basements, now or later, make sure you have enough room for stairs, including landing space at the top and bottom. For a 4-block-high wall (where the ceiling/next floor is at the fifth block), and a staircase that is 2 blocks wide, you will need an area that is 7 blocks long and 2 blocks wide.

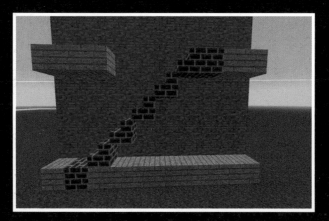

For simple 2-block-wide stairs, you'll need an area that is 7 blocks long and 2 blocks wide.

- **Front steps and porches.** If you want to add steps up to your entranceway or porches to the outside of your house, you will want to build a 2-block-high outline to show the walls and then fill in the interior with a choice of flooring, like wood planks. (If you want more than one level of steps up to your entryway, build your blueprint walls up to the height of the ground floor.)

- **Symmetry—odd or even.** If you want to place a single door or window in the center of a wall, you will need that wall to be an odd number of blocks long. If you want to place double doors in the center of a wall, the wall will need to be an even number of blocks long.

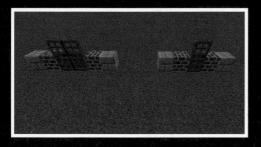

To center double doors along a wall, that wall will need to be an even number of blocks long. If you are centering a single door, the wall will need to be an odd number of blocks.

6. Review your blueprint.
Walk around your blueprint to see how you like it. Place some of your furniture in the outlined rooms to see where each piece will go. If you don't want to make and break furniture yet, use dirt blocks to show where things will fit. If you don't like something, redo your blueprint's mini walls until you are satisfied. Once you're happy, it's time to start building!

CHAPTER 4

BUILDING AND CUSTOMIZING YOUR SURVIVAL HOME

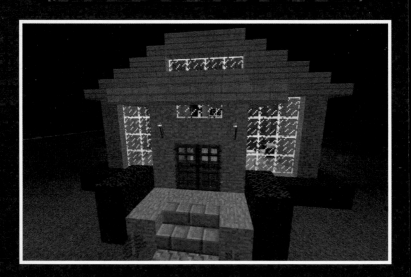

N ow that you have created a blueprint for your home, decided the number of floors, and chosen the style (if any) you'd like to use, you can begin building! Once your basic build is done, you can add and remove parts and blocks for detailing and realism. But start with your walls, floors, and ceilings.

1. Build up all your walls.
For windows, leave spaces or fill them in with a temporary block, like dirt, so that you don't have to break and recreate glass panes. I've used blue wool here.

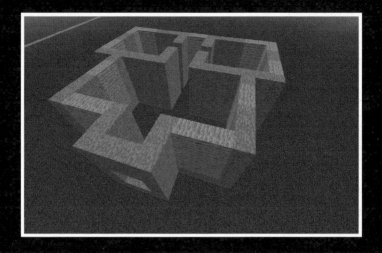

2. Dig out space for a basement.

If you want a basement, dig out at least 3 or 4 blocks deep. Place floor blocks. Replace the blocks underneath the blueprint walls with your basement wall blocks. Place a staircase to reach the ground floor or, when you fill out your ground floor in the next step, leave a hole for a ladder. Here, I've dug a massive basement to use for storage.

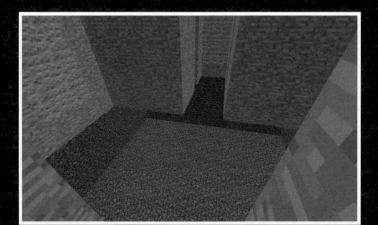

3. Fill out your floor.

Fill in your ground floor and add staircases or ladders to get to your basement, if you have one. Here, I've kept a hole for a ladder, and for the floor I've used the light birch wood and colored wool for carpet. Minecraft's carpet blocks are nice, but you can't put objects on top of carpet, so they are better used for open spaces where you won't place any furniture or objects like chests.

4. Build your upper stories.

If you have two or more stories, place the stairs up to this floor, fill out the floor, and place exterior walls for the second floor. Repeat for additional levels.

5. Add interior doors to rooms.

If you want doors to your rooms, add them. However, doors can be time-consuming to open and shut, and they require more building materials. You might want to have just having 1- or 2-block-wide entryways, if that works with your design.

6. Put a roof on your house.

There are many types of roof styles you can use. See chapter 7 for more roofing ideas. Here, I am building several low-pitched gabled roofs. Gabled roofs are sloped along two sides. Along the back section, the roof runs from left to right.

Atop the front section, the gable roof runs from front to back. I've adjusted it to have a flatter top. Over the entranceway, I've placed a hipped roof, sloping in at each exposed side. To create the shallow rise of all the roofs, I've used slabs of birch wood instead of full blocks. There was enough space to add clerestory windows (high windows, above eye-level) over the entrance-way roof.

Check the inside of your roof. You may want to make sure your ceilings are flat and that walls meet the roof, especially if you've used slabs instead of full blocks. Here, because I want an open feeling, I've extended the stone walls as high as they can go to the roof and filled in any extra half spaces with birch slabs.

7. Finish the entranceway.

Here, I've added steps, extended a block from the door, added torches, and used stone blocks at each side of the steps. I've also found room above the door for some more clerestory windows.

8. Decorate the interior.

In a small survival house, there's often not enough space for large furniture pieces, and you need most of the space for chests, furnaces, and a crafting table. Here, I've added some chairs made of white quartz, with item frames for arms. I've also placed item frames on chests as labels. The frame items show what's inside each chest.

9. Add landscaping.

Your house or building can look pretty bare if you don't do some minimal landscaping. A great easy look is to add leaf blocks around the bottom of the house as edging. Here, I've added leaf blocks around the foundation of the house and two birch trees with torches to light them. The path is made of gravel and stone for a textured effect and edged with ferns. Two fence posts hold torches for extra light.

CHAPTER 5

SIX HOME DESIGNS

You've probably built a dozen survival cabins or square homes. But there are so many styles of architecture that you can easily switch it up if you feel like a change. Here are six home styles that work well for smaller homes. You can copy any of these for a unique look and feel for your home in Minecraft or take ideas from them.

Georgian House

This is a very traditional Georgian home. Georgian architecture refers to a style of building in England between 1620 and 1720 during the reigns of four kings all called George. Most Georgian family homes share the following characteristics:

- Red brick with white columns and detailing
- One or two stories high, and one or two rooms deep

- Strictly symmetrical, with the front door centered and windows placed symmetrically

- Two chimneys, one on each side

- Door capped with a small window (transom) or decorative cornice

The Georgian home above uses the following materials:

- **Walls:** red brick with white quartz for detailing

- **Columns:** pillar quartz blocks and quartz block stairs

- **Window details:** brick stairs beneath windows, snow blocks for shutters

- **Roof:** Nether brick stairs

- **Chimney:** brick blocks with flowerpots

- **Entranceway:** details

Hobbit House

Hobbits are imaginary creatures—short, humanlike characters from the stories by J.R.R. Tolkien and featured in the book and movie *The Hobbit*. They live in cozy, semi-underground homes built into hills and banks, with rounded doors and windows. Although rounded windows and doors on a small scale aren't possible in Minecraft, you can make a cozy, earthy home tunneled into a hill. The door and windows should be the only non-dirt features on the outside. You can shape the hill into a rounded shape to show off the rounded features of hobbit houses.

Modern House

Modern houses come in many styles, but in general they feature flat surfaces, large expanses of windows, and lighter colors. Minecraft's square blocks mean that it is especially easy to create a realistic modern building. This modern structure uses clay, stone, quartz, and glass, with end rods for lighting. When you design a modern home, use different levels, corners, and insets to make the building interesting.

Earth Ship

Earth ships are earth-friendly homes built from natural and recycled materials, like tires filled with dirt and covered with plaster. They use passive solar power, which provides warmth by placing windows to catch the sun's rays. Many earth ships have curved, nature-like shapes and are built into a hillside. Mosaics are often used as a decoration because they can be built from broken tile and glass. Here, I've used emerald, lapis, and diamond ore for the mosaics and purple clay for the painted walls. A large, sloped, glass block window is placed to catch the sun during the day, while at night, end rods light up the interior space.

Art Deco Home

Art deco is a decorative and architectural style popular in the 1920s, '30s, and '40s. Art deco buildings emphasize the vertical and have stylized geometrical, zigzag, or sunburst elements. They often utilize glass blocks for windows, stucco exterior walls painted in light, pastel colors, and flat roofs. Art deco homes frequently have curved windows or walls, but you can still build an art deco home in Minecraft using pink clay, purpur pillars, white End stone brick, quartz blocks, End rods, and glass blocks.

Pueblo Home

Pueblo homes are found in the American Southwest, particularly in Arizona and New Mexico. These feature stucco or adobe walls in earth tones, wood columns, and flat roofs. The roofs often have low walls, or parapets, edging them. Roof beams and inset metal rain gutters extend past the exterior wall at the roof level. Here, I've used hardened clay, with spruce wood, wood fencing, and wood buttons for the extruding rain gutters. A clay chimney has two flowerpots on it to create the extending pipes.

CHAPTER 6

HOW TO DETAIL YOUR BUILDS

Most of us build our Minecraft homes simply. They are square or rectangular with straight, flat walls 3 or 4 blocks high and made completely out of brick or wood planks. To take your building to the next level and to make your homes both more exciting and realistic, follow the detailing principles that Minecraft building experts use.

Add Depth and Details

Add big or small insets, outsets or extrusions like pillars, and additional corners to your walls, whether they are perimeter walls or house walls. These create visual interest by breaking up the straight flat lines of a wall or a rectangular house. Here's an example of a wall with an extrusion (the wood pillars) and an inset (the chiseled stone blocks).

For example, you can add extra pillars to walls, use stair blocks to cap and base pillars, and add stone and wood buttons for extra details. When you are detailing, think about what elements you can add (or take away) at the top, bottom, and middles of walls—then experiment.

The basic process for adding details is to first construct your wall or building with its basic height and position.

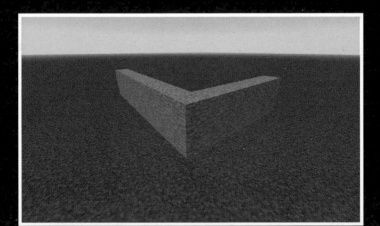

Then look at what types of details you can add at the bottom, middle, and top of the wall. Add and remove blocks as you experiment and create. Here, I've replaced some of the top of the wall with fencing and added stairs at the bottom. The pattern is repeated the whole length of the wall.

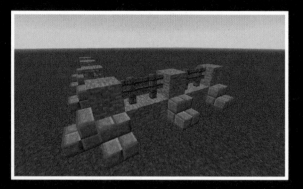

For more detailing, I've added torches to every other stone block column. To every stone block column, I've added stone buttons for extra depth.

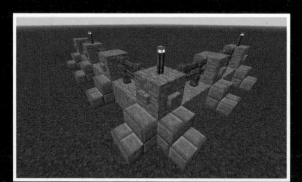

Blocks for Detailing

There are many blocks that Minecraft master builders use to detail their builds. When you are detailing, experiment with different colors, contrasting blocks, and patterns.

Common detailing blocks include: stairs, fences, leaves, slabs, ladders, buttons, iron bars, vines, glass panes, signs, item frames, flower pots, cobble and mossy cobble walls, and levers.

One caution: If you are using a redstone device for decoration, be careful not to place it somewhere it can be accidentally powered.

This wall uses stairs and slabs at the top, wood stairs at the bottom, and wood slabs in the insets. At the bottom of the insets are glowstone blocks, covered by leaf blocks.

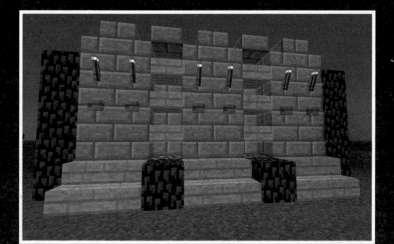

The Right Door

Choose the right door for your build. A dark oak wood door works well with traditional homes, iron doors are great for industrial and modern buildings, while a jungle or birch wood door will look better with more casual or summery builds. The spruce wood door is perfect with fantasy or medieval buildings.

There are seven different doors you can use to match or contrast with your building's style and colors.

Use Patterns

When you add detailing, use different types of block in a pattern to break up the monotony of using the same brick. A few blocks have sides that are different; you can change which side is shown by the way you place the block.

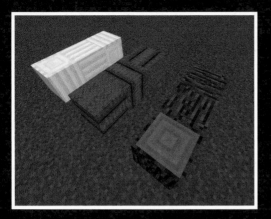

Pillared quartz, purpur pillars, hay bales, and all the raw wood blocks have three types of sides you can use in making patterns.

Here, a wall made of sandstone uses the three types of sandstone, along with extruded pillars, roof wall, and sandstone stair detailing. The pattern of blocks and columns is repeated all the way along its length.

Use Random Patterns

Sometimes you don't need a strict, repeated pattern to create interest. You can break up a flat expanse of wall, floor, or roof by adding blocks in a random pattern. This means you can't see a real pattern repeated. This often works best if the blocks you are using have some similarity. For example, on an ancient stone building, like the castle shown later in this book, you can use stone brick and place random blocks of cracked stone brick and mossy stone brick.

This modern wall has a random pattern using soul sand, black clay, brown clay, and brown wool.

Add Contrast

Using two different blocks that contrast can really help your building stand out. You can add contrast with different colors (red and blue clay), texture (fluffy gray wool and smooth shiny quartz), and darkness (dark wood and light wood).

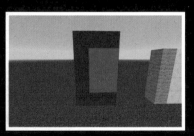

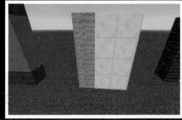

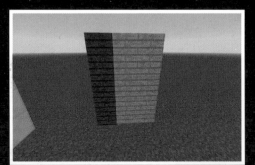

A common way to use contrast is to use a contrasting block to detail the corners of your buildings (almost as support pillars) and detailing around windows and doors. Here, a light birch wood is used for corners and detailing, and the main wall is made from the dark spruce wood block. Notice the different levels of depth by having the walls inset from the windows and pillars.

Use a Block Palette

If you have too many different blocks, colors, and textures in your build, it can look busy and unplanned. Master builders often create a block palette when they are planning. This is a set of at least three—and sometimes up to eight or so—blocks they will use for the build. The palette should include some blocks that complement each other and some that contrast or add texture. Notice how each has blocks that are similar color, with different texture, as well as some colors that are darker or different enough to provide contrast. A trip to the End will yield white End stone brick and bright purple purpur blocks, pillars, slabs, and stairs, which add a whole new dimension to your color palettes.

- Palette 1 (top): brick, pillar quartz block, quartz, chiseled quartz, red stained clay, nether quartz

- Palette 2 (middle): smooth sandstone, chiseled sandstone, sandstone, birch wood planks, pink stained clay, spruce wood planks

- Palette 3 (bottom): stone bricks, chiseled stone bricks, stone, spruce wood (raw), light gray wool, wool

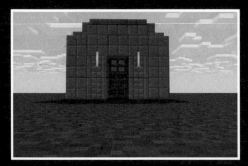

Purpur blocks come in block, stair and slab form. The End rod light shines as brightly

CHAPTER 7

DETAILING WINDOWS, ROOFS, FLOORS, AND MORE

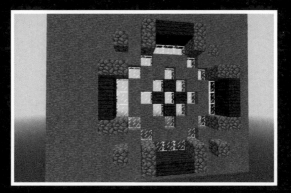

You can use the same basic principles we looked at in the last chapter to add detail and dimension to windows, stairs, paths and walkways, and roofs.

Windows

When you are detailing your building, look at ways your windows can add to the overall look. Some historic buildings work best with tall narrow windows, while modern buildings can look great with a large expanse of glass. Ways to add detail to windows include:

- Add stair blocks or other blocks above and below, or to the sides of the window.

- Inset or extrude the window from the wall.

- Add window boxes (make these out of dirt blocks surrounded by trapdoors).

- Instead of square windows, use arches, circles, crosses, or other shapes.

- Experiment with stained glass, glass blocks, and even fencing instead of glass.

Below are three windows showing what a difference detailing makes. At the right is a plain window using two glass blocks. The glass blocks make the surface of the wall totally flat.

In the middle window, you can see what a difference is made by just adding a stair block above and below and using glass panes. Glass panes add a level of depth to the flat wall.

And at the far left, the window area is entirely extruded by bringing the walls out. Extra stair blocks are added at the top for roofing, and leaf blocks bring in greenery, texture, and contrast.

Windows don't have to be square or use just glass. The diamond-like shape here is created using stair blocks. The nether fencing adds an extra layer of depth and contrast.

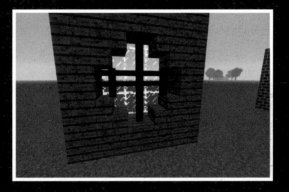

The arch of this window is extruded from the wall to add depth. It is made by placing stone brick stair blocks on whole stone brick blocks. The wall itself is detailed by placing cobble bricks randomly to give texture.

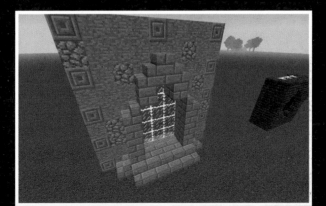

Paths and Walkways

Like walls, you can improve straight, single-block paths by adding
patterns and depth. You can use the same types of blocks you use
to detail walls. Elements to add to paths include:

- Use slabs, stairs, and different levels and materials
  for path borders and walls.

Lay out a natural-looking grass path, colored carpet, or other-
worldly purpur slab as a walkway.

- Raise the walkway height from the ground around
  it, or create a pattern by using half-slabs in place of
  some full blocks.

- Add arches or other coverings.

- Line a walkway with End stone and plant chorus
  plants to border either side of your path.

This pathway is raised and uses raw wood pillars at different
heights, joined by fencing to create visual interest and depth. The
wood blocks placed evenly along the walkway also visually break
up the flat expanse of wood.

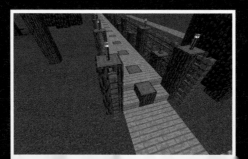

Depth and pattern in this stone brick walkway is added by using half-slabs at regular intervals along the pathway and stairs along the edges. Contrast is added by using stone brick, cobble, and chiseled brick.

Walkways don't have to be formal or use repeating patterns. Here's a stone pathway curving through the forest. I've placed cobblestone, mossy cobble, stone, and gray wool randomly to make the path look old and run-down. To light the path, I've embedded single glowstone blocks in the ground and covered them with bushes made of leaf blocks.

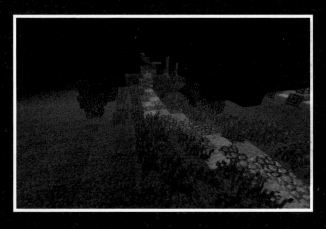

Stairs

The typical stair is a set of stair blocks using all the same material. But you don't have to stick to this. You can add landings and use slabs instead of stairs for a shallower slope. You can also use spiral stairs. Spiral stairs save space, although they make it more difficult to go up and down. You can even create a spiral Parkour staircase using End rods.

There are many ways to make spiral stairs. You can use stair blocks with slabs for landings or slabs alone. The stairs on the left are made from stair blocks and slabs, and the middle and right-hand stairs use slabs only. The stairs on the right also don't curve around a central column-like space; they simply run back and forth side-by-side.

As you can see, you can attach the step blocks around a central column or let them float. Single-block-wide spiral stairs take up the least amount of room but are the most difficult to climb up. If you don't have an enclosing wall for them, you can fall off them more easily.

Double-wide spiral stairs are much easier to climb. The stairs on the left curve around a 4-block-wide column and the ones on the right curve around a single-block column.

Plan your steps out so that you have 3 blocks of space above each step to allow you through!

Detail stairs by using different blocks for handrails or walls around the stairs. With 3-block-wide or wider stairs, you can also include different stair blocks for the steps. This stone brick stair is 3 blocks wide, so I've used wood stairs in the middle for contrast. I've used ladders on the outside as decoration. The stair walls are made from stone brick topped by fencing.

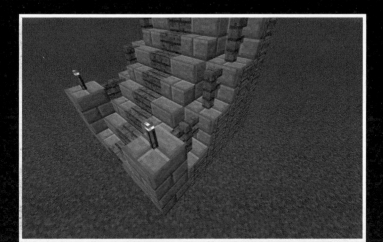

This simple wood stair uses slabs instead of stair blocks, which makes a less steep slope. I've used fencing for the handrail, and every other step has green carpet covering to add contrast.

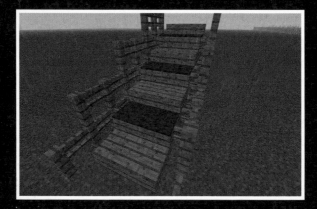

Floors

Experiment with all types of blocks for flooring. As with walls and walkways, you can repeat patterns with contrasting blocks, use a random pattern of similar blocks, and make patterns with the floor's height by using half-slabs.

If you have a large space to use up, you can make a large pattern, like this one below. It is a little like a parquet wood floor and uses four different wood planks.

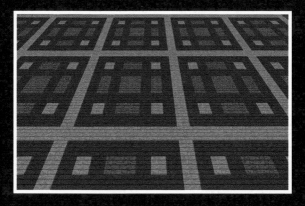

This floor uses different levels for depth and different stone blocks to add texture and pattern. The central square is made by placing steps around each other and adding a full height block in the center. Slabs are used for the cross pattern.

Roofs

Just as with walls, windows, floors, and stairs, you can use different blocks, textures, and colors to detail your roofs. First of all, you don't have to stick to using either a flat roof or the traditional gabled roof that slopes up along two sides to meet at the apex in the center. Other types of roofs are hipped roofs, shed roofs, saltbox roofs, and gambrel roofs.

A gabled roof slopes on two sides.

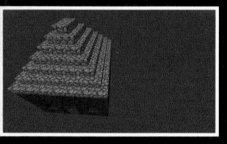

A hipped roof slopes on all sides, like a pyramid.

A shed roof slopes on just one side and is usually found on small buildings like sheds or extensions to a house.

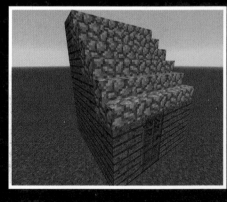

A saltbox roof slopes to a lower level on one side than the other. It's most commonly found on farmhouses.

A gambrel roof has a shallower pitch or slope at the top and a steeper pitch on the sides.

Other roofing techniques:

- Make the roofs steeper by using steep pitches (slopes).

- Make roofs shallower by using shallow pitches and slabs.

- Curve the roof by using the same types of slopes you use in circles and arches.

- Combine two types of roof. For example, you can combine a shed roof with a gabled roof.

Use the techniques you've learned with circles and arches to make curved roofs.

Centering Roofs

If you are using a sloped roof, take a look at how many blocks wide your building is. If it is an odd number of blocks wide, the top of your roof will be a single block, as on the left below. You won't be able to put a stair block at the top, but you can place a slab. If your building is an even number of blocks wide, you will have 2 blocks at the top and be able to place two stair blocks against each other.

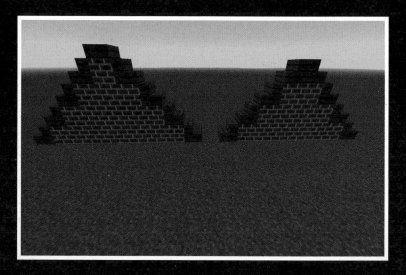

Detailing Roofs

For detailing roofs, you can use different types of stair blocks or slabs at different levels. You can add dormers and chimneys, as in the picture below. You can add depth by extending the roof out from the building.

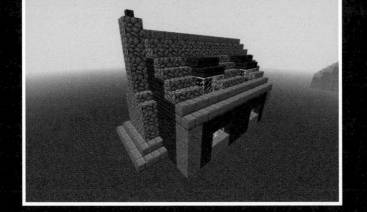

A flat roof can be detailed with different blocks and levels. This one uses chiseled stone, wood planks, cobblestone, stone, and stone slabs.

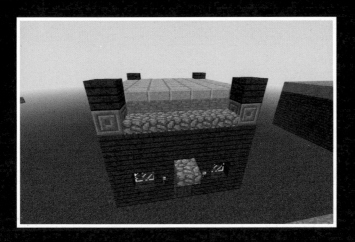

However, if your building is heavily detailed, it may be better to keep your roof fairly simple, so that it doesn't compete visually with the creativity of the walls.

CHAPTER 8

GLASS DOME

You can build a Minecraft biosphere in a desert with a glass dome—or, even better, with a series of glass domes connected by corridors. Because glass lets sunlight through, your farms will grow just as well inside a dome. If you keep the dome fully lit, you can also be completely protected from mobs. You can build your dome in any biome, but it's probably most impressive in a desert, mesa, or underwater.

Building a dome is the same thing as building a half sphere. You place increasingly smaller circles, one or more blocks deep, on top of each other. Follow the steps below to build a sphere that is 28 blocks in diameter. In these steps, I've used different colored blocks to help you see where to position the blocks, but you can build all the circles with glass blocks. If you have difficulty keeping track of the positions, you can build each new circle in a different color of block. Then, at the end, you can replace each block with a glass block.

One thing that can help in building circles and spheres is to concentrate on getting just one quarter of the circle right. Once that is done, you can copy the pattern to the other quarters of the circle.

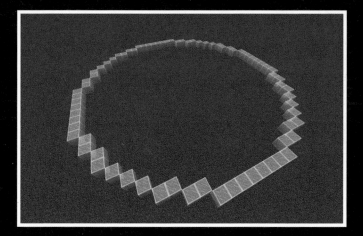

1. Build the first circle.
The first circle has "ends," or long sides, that are 8 blocks long. Each of the four curves begins and ends a set of 2 blocks connected by 3 single blocks in the center. Because the diameter of the dome is 28 blocks, the total height should be 14 blocks. However, to give some extra height, and to easily fit a door, we are adding an extra bottom circle.

2. Build the second and third circles.
Raise the first circle an additional 2 blocks for a total of 3 blocks of height.

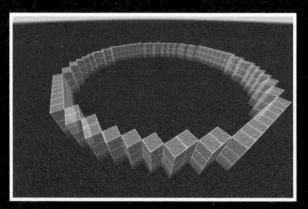

3. Build the fourth circle.
The fourth circle is very similar to the first three, but the long sides are only 6 blocks long, and the first set of blocks of the curve are 3 blocks long.

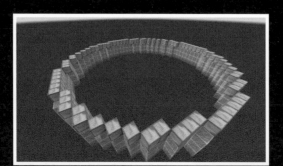

4. Build the fifth circle.

The fifth circle has ends or sides that are only 4 blocks long.

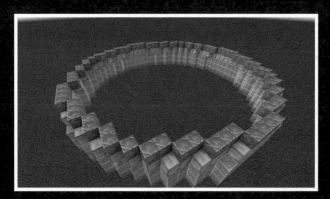

5. Build the sixth circle.

The sixth circle is the first one that is smaller in width (at the long ends) than the circles beneath. Notice how the long ends are 8 blocks long, and many of the blocks don't rest on a block beneath them.

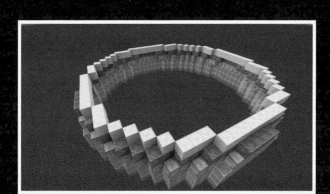

6. Build the seventh circle.
The seventh circle has long ends that are 6 blocks long.

7. Build the eighth circle.
The eighth circle is a block smaller or inside the circle beneath, with long ends that are 10 blocks long.

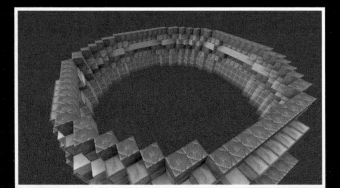

8. Build the ninth circle.
The ninth circle has long ends that are 6 blocks long.

9. Build the tenth circle.
This circle is also smaller than the ninth, with 8-block-long ends.

10. Build the eleventh circle.
The eleventh circle is also smaller than the previous, with 8-block-long ends.

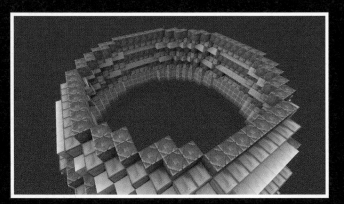

11. Build the twelfth circle.
The twelfth circle is smaller than the previous, again with 8-block-long ends.

12. Build the thirteenth circle.
The thirteenth circle has multiple blocks to create a flatter curve.

13. Build the fourteenth circle.
The fourteenth circle doesn't rest on any of the blocks of the circle below it.

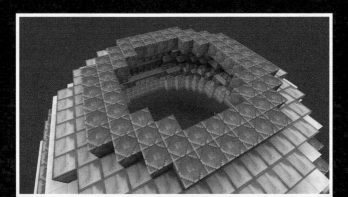

14. Finish the final circle.
The final circle is filled in. Like the previous circle, it doesn't rest on any of the blocks below.

15. Complete the dome.
If you have been using differently colored blocks to keep track of your circles, now is the time to replace all of the blocks with glass blocks. Add one or more doors and customize the interior as a house, garden, jungle, or animal pen. This dome below is customized as a jungle retreat and ocelot sanctuary. There are jungle trees, ferns, vines, bushes made of leaf blocks, a path, a bench, and, of course, ocelots!

CHAPTER 9

UNDERWATER HOME

hat could be cooler than an underwater base? On top of being pretty impressive, an underwater home gives you more protection from mobs and explosions than land-based homes. You can be sure a creeper isn't sneaking around outside! On the other hand, building underwater is harder than above ground, especially in Survival mode. Once your underwater home is built, you also have to be careful not to accidentally break an exterior wall block and flood your home. (If you do break a block, you can usually fill it pretty quickly with any other block for a temporary stopgap.)

There are a couple of good techniques for building an underwater home. In one, you build up walls from the ocean bottom, and in the other, you drop a sand mold onto the ocean floor. The first works better for shallower depths.

Underwater Building in Survival Mode

If you are building in Survival mode, there are several ways to help you breathe underwater.

- **Create air bubbles with blocks.** Several block types (fences, signs, doors, glass panes, iron bars, trapdoors, ladders) create an air bubble next to them. If you place these and stand next to them, you can breathe and replenish your air. If you are building very deep, you can create a pillar of sand and attach ladders to it. You can also place a torch to create a temporary air pocket, although the torch will immediately drop.

- **Emergency breathe with a bucket.** You can click an empty bucket in front of you. To reuse, click the bucket again to empty it.

- **Enchantments and potions.** Use a helmet with Respiration or Aqua Affinity or a Potion of Water Breathing.

Lighting the Depths

It can be very dark underwater, which makes it difficult to build. You can place glowstone blocks, sea lanterns, and jack o' lanterns to add light or use a Potion of Night Vision. You can also create a small "hut" of fences to enclose a torch on at least two sides and above. (The torch has to be placed last.)

Torches need air to stay alight, so you can use fences to surround a torch.

Method 1: Walls to Surface Mold

In this underwater building method, you create a blueprint or layout in dirt, above water, to show where your exterior walls will go. You can include walls that will form a tunnel from the land to your house.

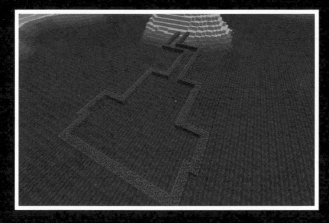

Here is a blueprint for th exterior walls o an underwater home, built on the ocean surface. The walls extend to the land, to help in building an underwater tunnel to the home.

You then build these walls down to the level where you want your floor to be. Use dirt blocks as you go down until you reach the ceiling. For example, if you want to have your ceiling 5 or so blocks below the surface, start with 5 dirt blocks. Then use the block you want for the ceiling. Then place wall or window blocks as far as your floor, and then the floor block. The floor block doesn't need to be on the ocean floor.

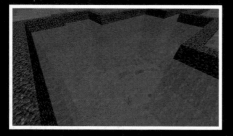

Here, you can see the walls built down, first with dirt to reach the ceiling level. Then glass blocks are used here for the walls and finally stone for the floor.

You then build in your floor, so you've essentially created a large tub, filled with water.

The floor is built in here with stone and glass to see through, because the floor is not on the sea floor.

If you don't want your home to look like it is floating, you can build pillars down to the ocean floor.

Back on the surface, drop sand or gravel blocks to fill up the interior of your house, all the way to the ocean surface. This clears the water from your home.

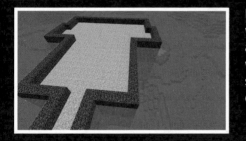

Here the interior is filled with sand. This removes air from the interior, and when you destroy the sand, the interior will be cleared of water.

Next, you break the sand or gravel, leaving air in its place. To quickly get rid of the sand, first dig down to the floor. Then break a floor-level sand block next to you and quickly fill the floor of that space with a torch. The torch will burn the sand falling above it.

Once the sand is removed, fill in the ceiling layer, including the ceiling of the entrance tunnel, if you have one. Back at land, make sure to build up steps to the surface.

This tunnel entrance has been enclosed with sandstone and a door.

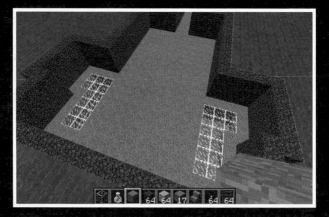

Filling in the ceiling, 4 blocks below surface level. Glass blocks will allow a little more light from the surface to get in.

Finally, you can break the temporary dirt walls, letting the water flow in above the house. Now you can enter your house from your tunnel and make any final changes. It is pretty easy to break a block and quickly fill it with another if you decide you want to change the look or you see a mistake.

The finished underwater house, with glowstone blocks used for lighting.

Method 2: Mold on a Platform

In this technique, first level the sea floor where you are placing the home. Above the water, build a temporary platform that is the width and length of your home. One way to start building right over the ocean, without a beam extending from the land, is to first place a lily pad block on the water.

You can place a lily pad on water and a block above that to start building.

Then you can place a dirt block over the lily pad as the start of your platform.

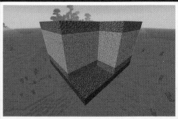

Build a mold of your home in sand or gravel on a platform. Here, the gravel shows what will eventually be the floor and roof.

When your platform is finished, build the shape of your home in gravel or sand. Make sure the home shape is all filled in. When you are satisfied, destroy the platform blocks so that the columns of sand or gravel drop down in place to land in position on the ocean floor.

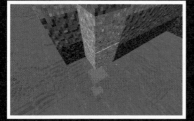

The sand or gravel mold will drop to the ocean floor when you destroy the platform it's on.

When you destroy the dirt platform, the sand and gravel mold drops to the sea floor. Then you need to swim underwater and place the exterior wall and roof blocks over the mold.

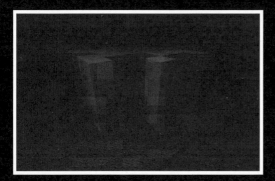

Here is the mold covered with walls and ceilings of sandstone and glass blocks for windows. The windows extend onto the ceiling as well for an overhead view.

You can use glass blocks for windows. Once the mold is sealed over, break in on one wall. Use a ladder to make an air space on the inside of the broken wall.

Place ladder blocks when you break into your house to create an air
space and prevent water from flooding in.

Then you can start destroying the sand or gravel blocks inside
your walls and roof. Once that is done, fill in your floor.

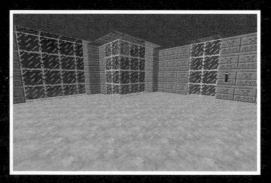

The finished home with floor filled in.

One way to make an exit is to place solid blocks, with ladder
blocks attached, all the way to the ocean surface. At the top,
you can make a landing with a dock or cove for a boat.

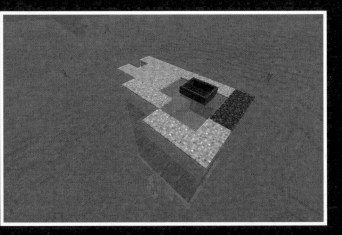

Here is a landing spot for the ladder entrance, with a sand cove (built on a dirt foundation) to hold a boat. You can use dirt blocks to seal off the cove to keep your boat safe.

CHAPTER 10
JAPANESE PAGODA

A pagoda is a building that typically has 3 or 5 stories and wide eaves that are often curved at the tips. Pagodas have been built in China, Japan, India, Vietnam, and other East Asian countries. They traditionally have been used for religious worship.

1. Build a raised foundation.
Build a raised foundation of stone or cobble that is 16x16 blocks square. Add steps in the center of one of the sides.

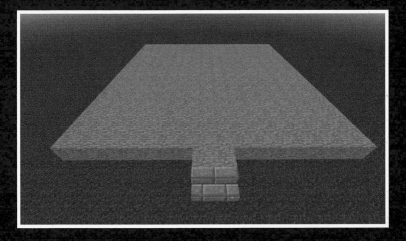

2. Build the first floor.

The building will be 10x10 blocks, with a 2-block entrance in the center of each of the four walls. Build the first floor in the center of the foundation. The floor is 4 blocks high. Use snow for the walls and red wool for the corner columns. Fill the top two rows in each entrance with one row of snow and a row of black wool.

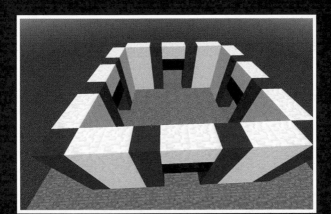

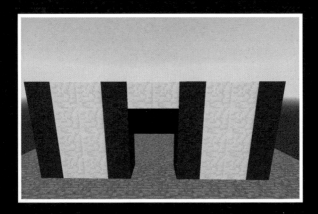

3. Add a cobblestone layer.
Top the first floor with a 1-block layer of cobblestone.

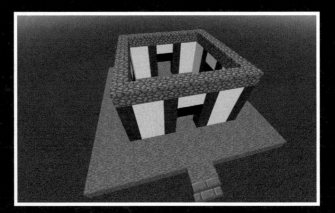

4. Build three more stories.
Build three more identical floors, using the first floor as your guide. Top each floor with a layer of cobblestone.

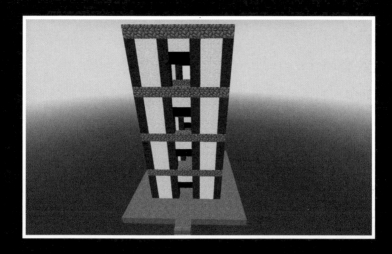

5. Add three roofs.
At each of the first three cobblestone layers of the building, build out a roof made of three levels of Nether brick slabs. Use a wood slab if you don't have access to Nether brick.

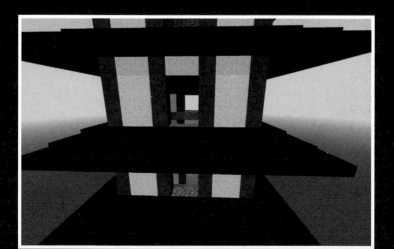

6. Add raised corners to the roofs.

Each roof is made of three levels of slabs. To build the raised corners of the pagoda roofs, first locate the outermost corner of the middle slab level. In this picture, this slab is the sandstone slab, just to show it clearly. From the level of slabs below this, remove the three slabs around it.

Next, add two slabs to the exposed sides of the corner slab. Use the same type of slab as the rest of the roof.

Lastly, add a slab in the empty corner, one slab level up as shown. (The slab is cobblestone in the picture to help show its position, but you should use the same roof slab as you've used elsewhere.)

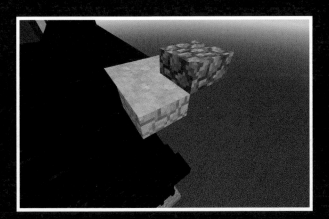

Repeat these steps for each corner of each roof.

7. Add entrance details.
At the pagoda entrance, add fence posts rising up and connecting to the roof with another slab. Fence in toward the entranceway and around the building. Add torches to the corners.

8. Add fence detailing on top of roofs.
On top of each roof and right next to the wall, place fence around the building.

9. Add fence detailing below each roof.

Beneath the roof, place fence all the way around the building. Attach the fencing to the second slab in. Add torches for light to the corners.

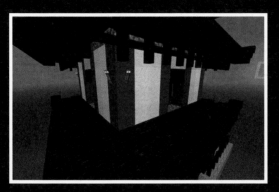

10. Begin building the top roof.

For the top roof, first build out from the cobblestone layer as you did with the three middle roofs, using three levels of slab. Add the same raised corners to the top roof as you did with the middle roofs.

11. Finish the top roof.

Next build inward. From the cobblestone base inward, use slabs for three levels, then use a slab topped with a stair block. The final level should be a solid block. Repeat this pattern on each side of the pagoda.

The final roof should look like this.

12. Customize your pagoda.

Inside your pagoda, you can add floors and decorate if you like. For a Japanese feel, surround your pagoda with a garden of birch trees, ponds and lily pads, wood walkways, and bridges. Here, the interior is decorated with lily pads in item frames, dead bushes in flower vases, and torches on Nether brick fence. You can make a traditional reed, or tatami mat, from hay bales. (You can use different faces of the hay bale block depending on how you click to place the bale.) In the center of the tatami mat is a special area (made of black wool) for a Japanese tea ceremony.

CHAPTER 11

FORTIFIED CASTLE

A fortified castle is a castle that has additional defensive features, such as a perimeter wall. Follow these steps to build an impressive castle with a barbican, or gated entrance building, and a defensive wall. You can adjust the measurements given to make the castle, towers, or walls bigger. The most important measurement is aligning the towers with each other so that connecting walls between them will run straight from one tower to the next.

1. Build four castle towers.

Each tower is 5x5 blocks square and 20 blocks high. The towers should form a square, with each tower 10 blocks from the next. Use colored wool to help you measure. As you build the castle, use a mix of stone bricks, cracked stone bricks, and mossy stone bricks. This will give the castle a timeworn appearance. You can substitute stone bricks with End stone brick for a warmer feel and lighter texture.

2. Build up the castle's walls.

Use the pattern below to build up the castle walls to 14 blocks high. The longest section of the wall is 5 blocks wide and has 2-block-wide sections at either side. The 2-block sections should be center aligned to the tower wall.

Select which of the four walls will be the front, and create an entranceway that is 4 blocks high and 3 blocks wide.

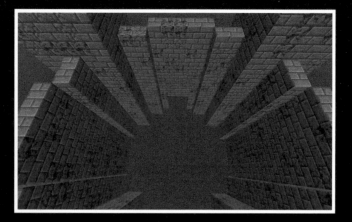

3. Plan the defensive wall.

The defensive perimeter of the castle will be four towers, connected by high walls with walkways. Use colored blocks to measure the center of each of the four towers, where the four towers will go, and to make sure they will line up with each other. Here, the corners where the center of the towers will be placed will be 18 blocks away from the front of the castle, 10 blocks from the sides, and 13 from the back.

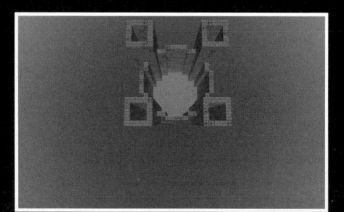

4. Build the outer towers.

Create the four outer towers, one at each corner, using the pattern below. The longest sides are 3 blocks wide. The center of the tower should be the same block as the red wool outline. Raise the towers 11 blocks high.

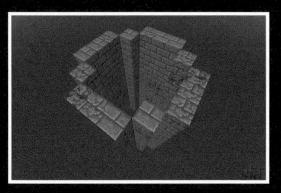

5. Roof each outer tower.

Roof each tower with a 7×7 platform. Add additional walls one block high, and one block out, on each side as shown.

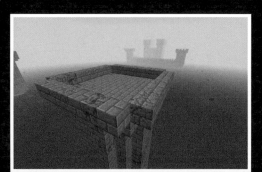

6. Add detailing to the tower.
Add upside-down stair blocks beneath the tower platforms.

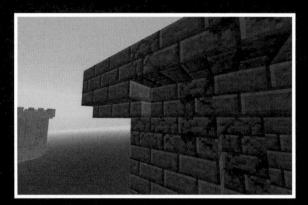

7. Build the barbican.
The barbican will provide entrance to the castle grounds. Build the barbican 11 blocks wide, 7 blocks high, and 6 blocks deep. It should be aligned with the two front towers and center aligned with the castle's entranceway.

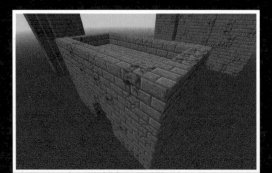

8. Create the barbican's entranceway.

Create an arched entry-way to the barbican as shown. It is 3 blocks wide and 3 blocks high, with upside-down stairs placed to create the arch.

9. Build the second circular section.

Add defensive walls between all four of the external towers and the barbican. The wall is made of two 5-block-high walls spaced 3 blocks apart. An upper walkway connects the two walls as shown.

10. Finish the castle towers.

On the outside of the four castle towers, add additional 5-block-wide by 4-block-high panels on each side at the top. These will meet diagonally at each side. These panels should extend higher than the inner wall by 1 block.

11. Finish the castle.

Add a roof to the castle, one block below the outer wall. Customize the interior as you like by adding floors, rooms, and halls.

12. Add crenellations.

Add crenellations by placing single blocks, spaced a block apart, to the tops of the castle towers, perimeter walls, and barbican.

13. Add windows.

Add evenly spaced, tall windows to the castle and the barbican, using iron bars to fill them in.

14. Add cobblestone paths.
Add a cobblestone path from the barbican to and around the castle. Add torches or End rods outside the castle entranceway and short columns with torches or End rods for the cobblestone path. Add iron bars around the inside frame of the castle door as a portcullis.

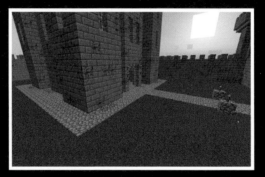

15. Add detailing to the barbican entrance.
Add iron bars for a portcullis at the inner and outer entrances of the barbican. Add columns with torches or End rods outside the outer entrance.

16. Customize the castle.

You'll now want to go through the castle, defensive walls and towers, and barbican to add rooms, floors, ceilings, staircases, ladders, and any more windows you want. This castle is customized with a moat and bridge just outside the perimeter wall.

CHAPTER 12

AIRSHIP

A irships were the first form of controlled and powered air transportation and were very popular in the early 1900s. Although there are quite a few types of airship, each uses a large bag filled with a gas that is lighter than air to fly. The bag is typically elongated, like the ellipsoids described in chapter 2, and a passenger cabin is attached to the bottom of the gas bag. Follow these steps to build your own airship.

1. Build the first frame.

Build the central frame for the balloon. First, use dirt to build a column at least 25 blocks high that will mark the bottom center of the balloon. Then build a cross as a frame for the center of the balloon. This frame will be used to build a circle later. Each of the four arms of the cross should be 6 blocks long. Use a different colored block to mark the circle's center. Here, I've used wood planks.

2. Build the second frame.
Build the center of the circle out horizontally with 10 blocks. I've used different wood planks to help in counting. Use the tenth block as the center to build the frame for a circle with four arms that are each 5 blocks long. I've used different colored wool for each crossed frame, to help distinguish each one, but you can use any blocks you like.

3. Build the third frame.
Build the central beam out another 3 blocks. Using the third block as a center, create a crossed frame with arms 4 blocks long.

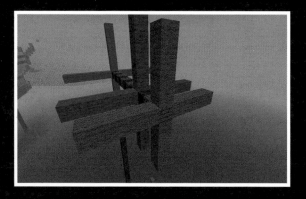

4. Build the fourth frame.
Build the central beam out another 3 blocks. With the third block as the center, build a crossed frame with arms 3 blocks long.

5. Build the fifth frame.
Build the central beam out another 2 blocks. On the last block, build a frame with arms 2 blocks long.

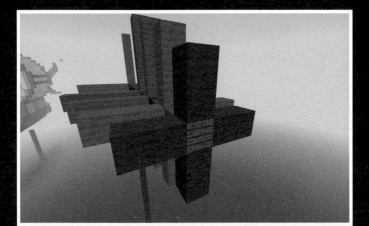

6. Build the sixth frame.

The sixth frame is right next to the fifth frame, with arms that are 1 block long.

7. Finish the framing.

Repeat steps 3 through 7 to build the frames for the other side of the balloon. The final balloon skeleton should look like the picture below. You can now use these frames to create circles, duplicating the circles in the same way as when you make a sphere. You can use this same process—building a series of frames for circles—for building ovoids of any size.

8. Build the first circle.

Build the first circle around the central frame as shown. The long sides of the circle, at the end of each arm, are 5 blocks long. Here, I am using colored wool to match the frame, but you can use white wool or any wool color you want for the finished balloon. The black wool blocks show where the circle touches at the end of the four frame arms.

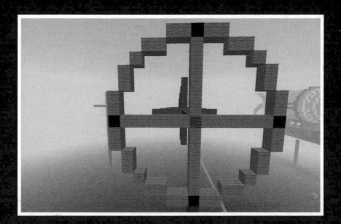

9. Build out the central circular section.

Extend this central circle on both sides 9 blocks out to the second frame on either side.

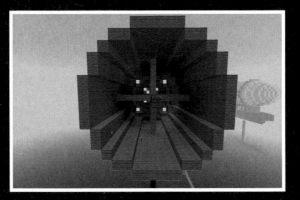

10. Build the second circular section.

On the second frame on each side, build a circle as shown and make it 3 blocks deep. The long side, at the end of each arm, is 5 blocks long.

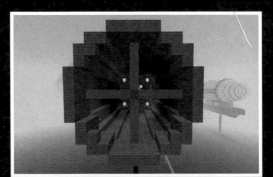

11. Build the third circular section.
Build the third frame's circle as shown and make it 3 blocks deep.

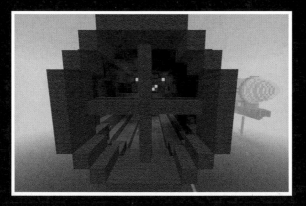

12. Build the fourth circular section.
Build the fourth frame's circle and make it 2 blocks deep. The long ends are 5 blocks long.

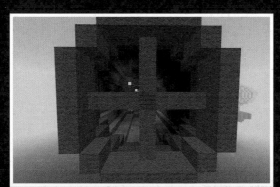

13. Build the fifth circle.

Build the fifth frame's circle as shown. The long ends are also 5 blocks long.

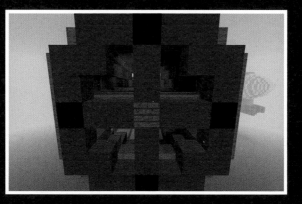

14. Build the sixth circle.

Build the sixth frame's circle. The long ends here are 3 blocks long.

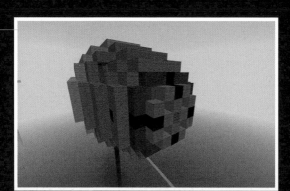

15. Fill in any gaps.
You may see that there are some holes in the surface. Fill these in so there are no gaps leading to the interior.

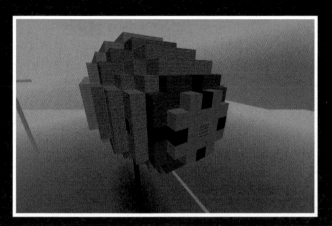

If you have used white wool for the balloon, it will look like the following figure.

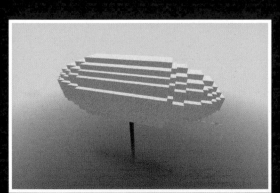

16. Add a frame to the balloon.

Now use wood blocks to create a frame around the balloon that will support the passenger cabin. The two screenshots show the side and the bottom of the frame.

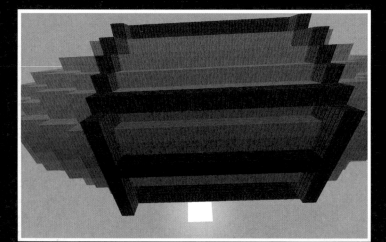

17. Add hanging supports.
Add 3-block-high columns at the four bottom corners of the balloon's wooden frame. The passenger "ship" will hang from these.

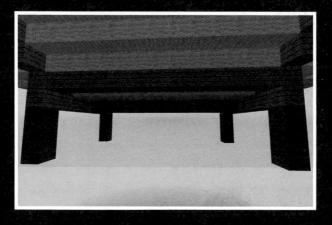

18. Shape the bottom of the ship.
On one end, build the outer shape of the ship.

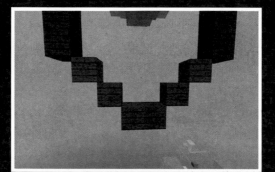

19. Build out the ship bottom.
Extend this ship to the two columns on the other end.

20. Create the curve for the ship's ends.
Build the curve for the end of the ship.

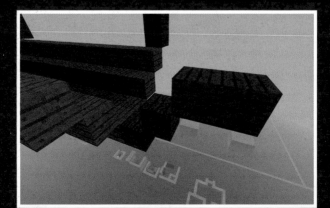

21. Build in the ship's end.
Complete the ship's end by filling in the blocks, curving toward the tip of the ship.

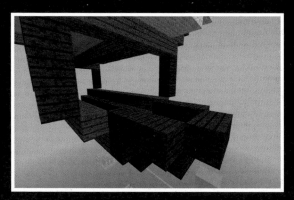

22. Build the other end of the ship.
Repeat this on the other end of the ship so that both ends of the ship are closed in.

23. Add a frame for a propeller.
First add a supporting frame made of wood blocks around one side of the ship as shown. Add a 2-block extension for attaching the propeller.

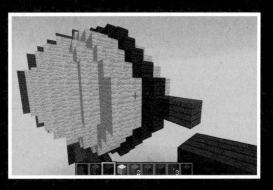

24. Build the base of the propeller.
Build out the propeller shape, 1 block deep in a dark wood plank.

25. Add detailing to the propeller.

On top of the base propeller shape, build the inner propeller shape, one block deep, in a lighter wood. Use dark wood for the center, and place a wood button in the center.

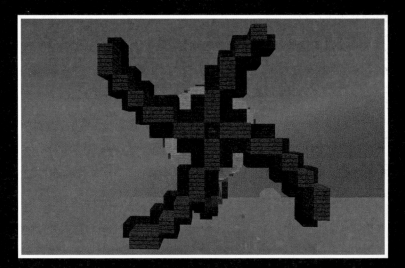

26. Customize your airship.

Finalize your airship by adding detailing, modifying the ship's shape, and installing lighting. Here, I've enclosed the center part of the airship and added a roof, windows, and doors. I added stair blocks for detailing and used fence posts for the airship's tether to the ground.

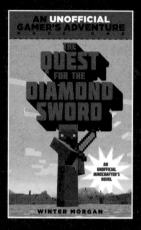

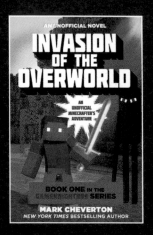